Tao

AND THE

City

Tao

AND THE

City

Lao Tzu's Tao Te Ching

Betsy Wyckoff

BARRYTOWN

STATION HILL

Published by Barrytown/Station Hill Press, Inc., Barrytown, NY, 12507, in conjunction with the Institute for Publishing Arts, Inc., a not-for-profit 501(c)(3) organization. The literary program is supported in part by grants from The New York State Council on the Arts.

Web: http://www.stationhill.org
Email: publishers@stationhill.org

Cover design by Susan Quasha
Typesetting and text design by Betsy Wyckoff

Library of Congress Cataloging-in-Publication Data

Wyckoff, Betsy.
  Tao and the city : Lao Tzu's Tao te ching / Betsy Wyckoff.
     p. cm.
  ISBN 1-886449-48-1
  1. Laozi. Dao de jing. 2. Taoism. I. Title: Lao Tzu's Tao te ching.
II. Title.

  BL1900.L35W9 2003
  299'.51482—dc21

                                        2003006203

Contents

Preface

Historically, Taoism, Confucianism, and Buddhism were major influences on Chinese thought. Of the three, Taoism is least well known in the West. The *Tao Te Ching* was written by Lao Tzu. A contemporary of Confucius, Lao Tzu was born in China in 604 B.C., according to some scholars.

The *Tao Te Ching* sometimes is translated as "The Way and Its Virtue." In the *Tao Te Ching,* Lao Tzu tells us how to achieve balance and harmony—how to become one with nature. It is a meditation on life.

Like all sacred writings, the *Tao Te Ching* can be read again and again. New insight comes with each reading. For anyone interested in spirituality, the *Tao Te Ching* is like a well of spring water that continually refreshes.

My goal in writing *Tao and the City* is to achieve simplicity, clarity, and updated language while remaining faithful to the themes presented in the original Chinese.

The photographs in this book are my interpretation of a Tao-inspired art form. I took all of the photographs in New York City with the exception of the blue photographs on pages vi and 80, which I took in a glass bathhouse in Hamilton, Bermuda.

BETSY WYCKOFF

New York City

Tao

AND THE

City

1

The tao that can be named is not the real Tao.
The name that can be put into words is not the real Name.

The unnameable is the origin of heaven and earth.
The Named is the mother of the ten thousand things.
The ten thousand things are all things existing in the world.

Without desire, the mystery can be realized.
With desire, you see only the surface of things.

Yet these two together arise from the same source.
They are the mystery of mysteries.
They are the gateway to spirituality.

2

When everyone recognizes beauty as beauty, ugliness is born.
When everyone recognizes the good as good, evil is born.

Therefore, being and nonbeing define each other.
The difficult and the easy produce each other.
The long and the short contrast with each other.
Above and below complete each other.
Sound and voice depend on each other.
Before and after distinguish each other.

The sage acts with nonassertion and teaches by silence.
The ten thousand things arise and are not refused.
They are acted upon without being dwelled on.
Tasks are accomplished without seeking merit.
The sage creates but does not possess.
Actions are taken and then let go.
Once let go, they last forever.

3

Not to exalt the worthy prevents people's envy.
Not valuing rare treasures prevents people from stealing.
Not displaying the desirable helps people remain undisturbed.

Therefore, the sage governs the people by emptying their hearts
and filling their bellies.
The sage weakens their ambition and strengthens their bones.
The sage keeps the people unsophisticated and without desire.
In this way, the crafty do not dare to act.
Practicing nondoing, everything is in order.

4

The Tao is like an empty bowl.
In being used, it can never be exhausted.
Bottomless, it is the ancestor of the ten thousand things.

It will blunt the sharpness.
It will untangle the knots.
It will dim the glare.
It will be one with the dust.

It is hidden but ever present.
Its parents are not known.
It seems to have preceded the gods.

5

Heaven and earth are impartial.
They view the ten thousand things as straw dogs.
The sage is impartial.
The sage views the people as straw dogs.

The space between heaven and earth is like a bellows.
It is empty but inexhaustible.
The more it moves, the more comes forth.

After much talk there is silence.
Hold fast to the void.

6

The source of the fountain never dies.
It is called the mysterious woman.
The gateway of the mysterious woman is the root of heaven and earth.
It endures forever.
Use it and you will find it inexhaustible.

7

Heaven and earth endure and are everlasting.
Why is this so?
Because they do not live for themselves they can exist forever.

By remaining in the background the sage comes to the foreground.
By surrendering self-concern the sage's self-concern is preserved.
By becoming selfless the sage finds fulfillment.

8

The highest good is like water.
It benefits the ten thousand things but does not compete with them.
Because water dwells in places most people shun, it finds the Way.

When building a dwelling, keep close to the ground.
In thinking, value profound thoughts.
In friendship, value gentleness.
In speaking, value truth.
In government, value order.
In work, value competence.
In action, value timeliness.

Without competition there is no reproach.

9

Keep filling the cup and it will overflow.
Keep sharpening the blade and it will become blunt.
An abundance of gold and jade cannot be protected.
Riches, status, and pride bring disaster.
To stop when the work is done is heaven's way.

10

Can you keep body and spirit together without separating them?
Can you concentrate your vital energy and become supple as a
newborn?
Can you cleanse and purify your intuition to be free from faults?
Can you love the people and govern the state practicing
nonassertion?
Can you open and close the gates of heaven playing the feminine
role?
Can you penetrate the four quarters without taking any action?

Giving birth and nourishing,
bearing but not possessing,
acting without expectations,
and leading but not controlling.
All are profound virtues.

11

Thirty spokes unite in a wheel.
Their utility is dependent on the hole at the center of the wheel.
Clay is molded to form a vessel.
Its utility is dependent on the hollowness of the vessel.
Doors and windows form a house.
Their utility is dependent on the empty space within the house.

Existence yields the actual.
Nonexistence yields what is useful.

12

All colors combined confuse the eye.
All sounds combined make only noise.
All tastes combined would be offensive.

Without discrimination all is chaos.

The sage distinguishes the fundamental from the superficial.
The sage focuses on the former, not the latter.

13

Favor bodes disgrace and causes trembling.
High rank, like the body, leads to heartache.

What is meant by saying favor bodes disgrace and causes trembling?
The acquisition of favor causes trembling.
The loss of favor causes trembling.
This is what is meant by saying favor bodes disgrace and causes trembling.

What is meant by saying high rank, like the body, leads to heartache?
I suffer heartache because I have a body.
Without a body there is no heartache.

Therefore, I can be trusted to govern the world
if I value the world as I value my body.

14

We look at it and find it formless.
We listen to it and find it soundless.
We reach for it and find it cannot be held.

These three things cannot be analyzed.
They flow into one.
The one has no shape or substance.
It is unnameable and returns to nonexistence.

Formless and imageless, it is beyond description.

From the front it has no beginning.
From the back it has no end.

Follow the ancients and the present can be mastered.
Follow the ancients and the origin of the past can be understood.
This is the essence of the Tao.

15

The ancient masters were subtle, mysterious, and profound.
We can never understand the depth of their knowledge.
All we can do is describe their appearance.

They were as cautious as people crossing a winter stream.
They were as alert as people fearing danger.
They were as courteous as guests.
They were as yielding as ice melting.
They were as simple as uncarved wood.
They were as empty as a valley.
They were as obscure as a troubled pool.

The ancient masters could clarify muddy waters.
They could stir the still.

Because they did not seek fulfillment, they did not wear out.
They were beyond the need for renewal and were complete.

16

We should try our utmost to achieve emptiness.
Tranquillity will be found at the center.

The ten thousand things arise and bloom.
They flourish and return to their root.
Returning to the root brings stillness.
At the root is the eternal.
Knowing the eternal is enlightenment.
From not knowing the eternal passion arises.
Following passion leads to tragedy.

Knowing the eternal the mind opens.
With an open mind one will be openhearted.
To be openhearted is to act kingly.
Acting kingly is to attain the divine.
Attaining the divine is to attain the Tao.
Though the body dies, the Tao lives forever.

17

People barely notice the existence of great rulers.
Next come rulers people praise.
Still lesser rulers people fear.
The worst rulers people despise.

If your trust be insufficient, you will receive no trust.

Great rulers select their words with care.
They accomplish their work
so that the people say, "We did it ourselves."

18

Without the Tao
we need the concepts of humanity and righteousness.
With cleverness and knowledge
there comes great hypocrisy.
When family relations no longer matter
we need the concepts of piety and paternal devotion.
A country in chaos
gives rise to loyalty and patriotism.

19

Give up saintliness, abandon cleverness,
and the people will gain a hundredfold.

Give up benevolence, abandon righteousness,
and the people will return to family devotion and love.

Give up shrewdness, abandon profit,
and thieves and robbers will no longer exist.

These three things are externals and are insufficient.
In addition, we must:
Treasure that which will endure,
seek simplicity, preserve the genuine,
diminish the self, and reduce desire.

20

Is there a distinction between yes and no?
Is there a distinction between good and evil?
Must I fear what others fear?

The people are joyous, as if at a feast.
I am quiet, not having received any sign.
I am like an infant before it has learned to smile.
I am weary and have no home.

Others have enough but I have nothing.
I am a fool who is confused.
Others are bright but I am dim.
Others are sharp but I am dull.
I drift on the ocean without direction.
Others have a purpose but I have no aim.

I am different from the others.
I am nourished by the Tao.

21

People of virtue follow the Tao.

The Tao is vague and elusive.
Although vague and elusive, within it is form.
Although vague and elusive, within it is substance.

Shadowy and dim, it contains an essence.
Within this essence lies faith.

The Tao has lasted throughout time.
How can we explain its origin?
Through what is within us.

22

The crooked shall be made straight.
The crushed shall be made whole.
The empty shall be filled.
The worn shall be renewed.
Those who have little will gain much.
Those who have much will become confused.

Therefore, the sage embraces the Tao
and becomes a model for the world.

Not making a show, the sage shines forth.
Not self-justifying, the sage becomes prominent.
Not self-asserting, the sage receives credit.
Not self-seeking, the sage endures.
Not competing with anyone, no one competes with the sage.

The crooked shall be made straight
and the straight shall return home.

23

To be quiet is natural.
High winds do not last all morning.
A cloudburst does not last all day.
Heaven and earth produce these events.
If heaven and earth cannot make these events eternal, how can man?

A person who follows the Tao is at one with the Tao.
A person who pursues virtue is at one with virtue.
A person who experiences loss is at one with loss.
A person at one with the Tao finds a welcome companion in the Tao.
A person at one with virtue finds a welcome companion in virtue.
A person at one with loss finds a welcome companion in loss.
Without sufficient faith, there is no faith.

24

Standing on tiptoe leads to unsteadiness.
To straddle is to stumble.
To display oneself is to lack enlightenment.
To assert oneself is to lack distinction.
To boast of oneself is to lack merit.
To brag of oneself is to lack endurance.

From the point of view of the Tao,
these things are like excessive food and useless baggage.
Followers of the Tao avoid them.

25

There is an entity wondrous and mysterious.
It was born before heaven and earth were formed.
It can be found in the silence and the void.
It stands alone and does not change.
It is always in motion.
It does not suffer.
It is the mother of the ten thousand things.

I do not know its name.
I call its nature "The Tao."

Forced to give it a name, I would call it "The Great."

It flows to the beyond and then returns home.

The Tao is great, heaven is great,
the earth is great, and royalty is great.
Royalty is included in the four great things.

Humanity's model is the earth.
Earth's model is heaven.
Heaven's model is the Tao.
The Tao's model is its essential nature.

26

The heavy is the root of the light.
The tranquil is the root of activity.

Traveling all day,
  masters must not lose sight of their baggage.
Faced with glorious sights,
  they must remain detached and tranquil.

How should the ruler govern the empire?
To be too light is to lose one's subjects.
To be too active is to lose the throne.

27

A good traveler leaves no tracks.
A good speaker talks without fault.
A good counter needs no measuring stick.
A good door needs no lock, yet it cannot be opened.
A good binding needs no knot, yet it cannot be untied.

The sage takes care of all the people, excluding no one.
The sage takes care of all things, excluding nothing.
This is called practical enlightenment.

The good person teaches the bad.
The bad person is the charge of the good.
One must revere one's teacher.
One must value one's charge.
Not to do so is to be on the wrong road.
This is the essence of the Tao.

28

Know the strength of the masculine
but retain the care of the feminine.
Be like a river in the world.
Being like a river in the world,
never deviate from the path of virtue.
Thus, become like a little child.

Let your brightness shine
but also accept your dullness.
Become a model to the world.
Becoming a model to the world,
never lose sight of virtue.
Thus, return home to the absolute.

One who knows glory but keeps humble
nourishes the world.
To nourish the world
is to be sufficient in virtue.
Thus, returning to a state of simplicity.

When diversified, simplicity becomes a vessel of usefulness.
By using it, the sage becomes a leader.
Thus, a great principle becomes universal.

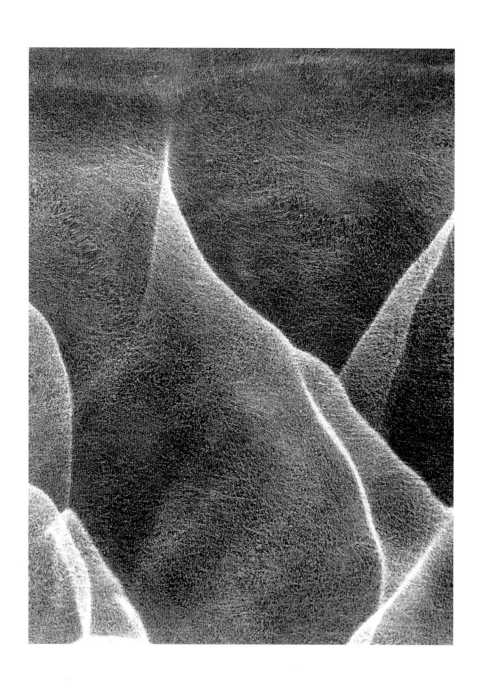

29

Trying to improve the universe
does not lead to success.
The universe is sacred and cannot be improved.
Trying to change it leads to ruin.
In trying to grasp it, you lose it.

It is said of human beings:
Some are compliant, some are bold.
Some breathe warmly, some coldly.
Some are strong, some are weak.
Some are up, some are down.

Therefore, the sage avoids excess,
the sage avoids extravagance, and
the sage avoids extremes.

30

One who advises a ruler in the way of the Tao
will not advise the use of force.
The use of force invites retaliation.

Thorns and briars grow where armies are stationed.
Famines follow in the wake of war.
A good person acts with determination and then desists.

Be determined but do not boast.
Be determined but do not be proud.
Be determined but do not be arrogant.
Be determined because it is unavoidable.
Be determined without using violence.

When things flourish and then decay,
they are not following the Tao.
Not to follow the Tao is to perish.

31

Even weapons used in victory are evil.
The person who possesses Tao shuns them.

When at home the righteous person turns to the left.
When at war the righteous person turns to the right.

Weapons are instruments of evil.
They are not the tools of the righteous person.
When peace and quiet are valued,
weapons are used only when unavoidable.

The righteous person does not rejoice over a victory.
To rejoice over a victory is to enjoy the slaughter of others.
One who enjoys the slaughter of others
will not thrive in the empire.

Slaughter in war should be treated with sorrow and grief.
Every victory is a funeral rite.

32

The Tao is eternal and nameless.

Although its simplicity seems slight, none can grasp it.
If princes and kings could hold onto it,
the ten thousand things would pay homage.
Heaven and earth would unite to send forth sweet dew.
The people would unite with no need of command.

Forming systems requires names.
At some point, it is time to stop acquiring names.
Knowing when to stop naming helps one avoid danger.

The Tao's relation to the world
is like a river flowing into the sea.

33

To know others is to be skilled.
To know oneself is to be enlightened.

To conquer others is to be forceful.
To conquer oneself is to be strong.

To know contentment is to be rich.
To persevere is to have purpose.

To keep one's place is to endure.

To die but not to perish is to live forever.

34

The Tao flows everywhere.
It flows to the left.
It flows to the right.

The Tao gives life to the ten thousand things.
It never refuses them.
When its task is finished, it does not expect credit.
The Tao nourishes the ten thousand things
but does not claim mastery over them.

Without desire, the Tao is classed with the small.
The ten thousand things call it home
but are not ruled by it.
Thus, it can be classed with the great.

Although not seeking to be great,
the Tao accomplishes greatness.
The sage, too, accomplishes greatness
by not seeking to be great.

35

All the world will come to those who follow the Tao.
They will suffer no harm but rather
will find peace, shelter, and rest.

Music and good food beckon to us.
But the Tao has no sound or taste.
When looked at it cannot be perceived.
When listened to it is inaudible.
However, when acted upon, the Tao is inexhaustible.

36

That which is shortened must first be lengthened.
That which is weakened must first be strengthened.
That which is fallen must first be raised.
That which is received must first be given.

The weak conquers the strong.
The soft conquers the hard.

Fish must not leave the water.
Rulers must not display their weapons.

37

The Tao practices nonaction,
yet nothing is left undone.

If princes and kings practiced the Tao,
the ten thousand things would be reformed.
If having been reformed they desire to act,
they would be restrained by the simplicity
of that which is nameless.

The simplicity of the nameless would purify desire.
Without desire there would be tranquillity and peace.

38

People with superior virtue are not aware of their virtue.
Therefore, they possess the greatest virtue.
People with inferior virtue never lose sight of their virtue.
Therefore, they have no virtue.

People with superior virtue take no action and are without
pretension.
People with inferior virtue take action and are pretentious.

Truly kind people act but have no pretension.
People guided by justice act and are pretentious.

People conversant in ritual act, and when no one responds,
they resort to persuasion by force.

Thus, without Tao, virtue appears.
Without virtue, kindness appears.
Without kindness, justice appears.
Without justice, ritual appears.
Ritual, the mark of loyalty and faith, is the beginning of disorder.

Knowledge of the future, the flower of the Tao,
is the beginning of folly.

Truly great people concentrate on what is internal,
not what is on the surface.
They concentrate on the fruit, not the flower.
Therefore, discard the flower and retain the fruit.

39

From ancient times these things have attained oneness:

Sky by oneness becomes clear.
Earth by oneness becomes steady.
Spirit by oneness becomes holy.
Valleys by oneness become full.
Creatures by oneness become alive.
Kings by oneness become rulers.
Such is the virtue of oneness.

If the sky was not clear, it would tear.
If the earth was not steady, it would break into pieces.
If the spirit was not holy, it would be deceased.
If the valleys were not full, they would become used up.
If creatures were not alive, they would become extinct.
If kings were not rulers, they would fall.

Nobles find their roots in the common.
The humble is their foundation.
Princes and kings describe themselves as
"orphaned," "worthless," and "lonely."
The humble is their foundation.

The parts of a carriage cannot in and of themselves be called
a carriage.

The one who is unified seeks not to be praised like a gem
but to be strong like stone.

40

The Tao flows toward home.
Yielding is the way of the Tao.

The ten thousand things come from being
and being comes from nonbeing.

41

When wise people hear of the Tao they practice it.
When average people hear of the Tao they half accept it.
When foolish people hear of the Tao they ridicule it.
If it were not ridiculed, it would not be the Tao.

Therefore, the poet says:
The bright way seems dim.
Going ahead seems like going back.
The smooth seems uneven.

The highest virtue seems hollow.
The greatest purity seems soiled.
The most steadfast virtue seems insufficient.

Solid virtue seems transparent.
Firm substance seems changeable.
The perfect square has no corners.

Great talent is slow to mature.
Great sound is hardly heard.
Great form has no shape.

The Tao is hidden and nameless.
It provides for all and brings forth fulfillment.

42

The Tao produces unity.
Unity produces duality.
Duality produces trinity.
Trinity produces the ten thousand things.

The ten thousand things are nourished by yin
and embraced by yang.
These opposites unite to form the absolute.

Although people feel orphaned, lonely, and unworthy,
royalty selects these feelings as their titles.
Thus, some people lose by gaining,
other people gain by losing.

What others teach, I also teach:
The violent die a violent death.
This is the basis of my belief.

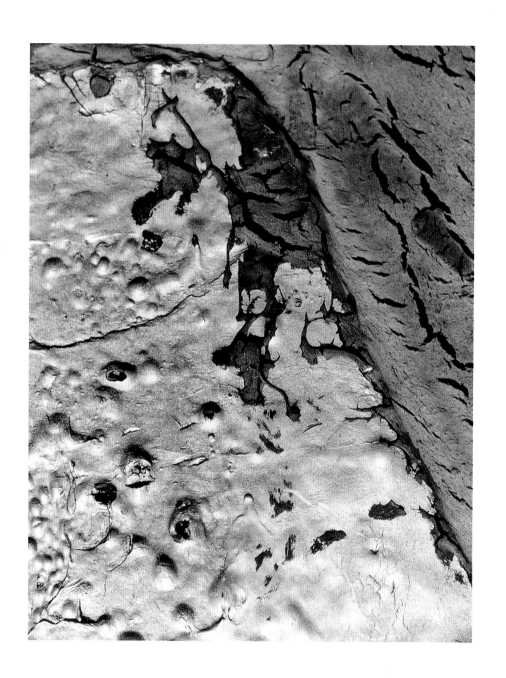

43

The softest overcomes the hardest.

Nonexistence fills the impenetrable.

By this I comprehend nonassertion.
Few understand the benefit of nonassertion
and the beauty of silence.

44

Which is more important: Fame or self?
Which is more valuable: Self or fortune?
Which is more harmful: Gain or loss?

Great desire leads to extravagant spending.
Hoarded wealth invites theft.

Contentment incurs no disappointment.
Knowing when to stop avoids danger.
In this way one endures forever.

45

Great perfection has flaws.
Its usefulness is inexhaustible.
Gratefulness seems empty.
Its usefulness is endless.

Straight lines look bent.
Great skill appears clumsy.
Great eloquence resembles stammering.

Movement keeps us warm.
Stillness keeps us cool.
Quietness and serenity are the norm.

46

When the world is in possession of the Tao,
farm horses plow the fields.
When the world is not in possession of the Tao,
war-horses appear on the border.

There is no greater crime than desire.
There is no greater evil than discontent.
There is no greater misfortune than greed.

Therefore, one who knows what is enough
will always be content.

47

Without going out-of-doors,
one may know the whole world.
Without looking through the window,
one may know the way of heaven.
The further one goes, the less one knows.

The sage knows without traveling,
sees without looking,
and achieves without labor.

48

One who seeks learning will grow day by day.
One who seeks the Tao will diminish day by day.
One continues to diminish until arriving at nonassertion.

With nonassertion everything can be achieved.
By letting go one gains the world.
By interfering one loses the world.

49

Masters do not have hearts of their own.
The hearts of their communities become their hearts.

One meets good with goodness.
One also meets bad with goodness.
In this way one obtains goodness.
One meets the faithful with faith.
One also meets the faithless with faith.
In this way one obtains faith.

Masters are humble in dealing with the world.
Their hearts encompass the universe.
Communities look and listen to their masters.
Masters care for their communities
as they care for their own children.

50

We go forth in life and come home in death.

Three in ten travel toward life.
Three in ten travel toward death.
The remainder exist beyond life and death.
Why do some move into the realm of death?
Because they excessively strive after life.

One whose life is based on goodness
will not fall prey to rhinoceroses or tigers.
One whose life is based on goodness
will not fall prey to the weapons of soldiers.
One will not be gored if rhinoceroses
have no place to thrust their horns.
One will not be torn apart if tigers
have no place to use their claws.
If there is no place for weapons to enter,
there is no place for death to enter.

51

The Tao gives life to all creatures.
Virtue nourishes all creatures.
Matter gives form to all creatures.
Community gives shape to all creatures.
The ten thousand things respect the Tao and honor virtue.

They have not been ordered to respect the Tao and honor virtue
but do so spontaneously.

The Tao gives life to all creatures.
Virtue nourishes them, raises them, nurtures them,
completes them, matures them, supports them, and
protects them.

To give life but not to own it,
to create but to take no credit,
and to guide but not to master
are the most profound virtues.

52

At the beginning of the world,
the Tao was the world's mother.

As children know their mothers,
the mothers know their children.
As mothers hold onto their children,
the children hold onto their mothers.
In this way, the children are never in danger.
Those who close their mouths and guard their senses
will encounter no trouble in life.
Those who open their mouths and meddle with affairs
cannot be saved.

Those who perceive the small are enlightened.
Those who yield to tenderness are strong.
Those who practice the Tao and are enlightened
will not have to face spiritual ruin.
This is called following the eternal.

53

Were I to have even a little knowledge,
I would walk on the path of the Tao.
My only fear is that I would go astray.

The route of the Tao is very straight
but people are fond of byways.

When the palace is splendid
the fields contain weeds
and the granaries are empty.

To wear ostentatious clothing,
to carry sharp swords,
to excessively eat and drink, and
to have an abundance of costly possessions
is thievery.

Surely, thievery is not the way of the Tao.

54

What is firmly planted cannot be uprooted.
What is firmly grasped cannot be lost.
It will be honored throughout the generations.

Cultivate virtue in the self and it will be genuine.
Cultivate virtue in the family and it will overflow.
Cultivate virtue in the township and it will be long lasting.
Cultivate virtue in the country and it will be abundant.
Cultivate virtue in the world and it will be universal.

The self must examine the self.
The family must examine the family.
The township must examine the township.
The country must examine the country.
The world must examine the world.

How do I know this is so?
By looking within.

55

They who are filled with virtue
are like newborn babies.

Wasps and vipers do not sting them.
Wild beasts and birds of prey do not attack them.
Although their bones and muscles are weak,
their grip is strong.
They may be virgins but they are sexually vital.
They cry and sob without growing hoarse.
They are in perfect harmony.

To be in harmony is to be eternal.
To be eternal is to be enlightened.

To force the growth of life is a bad omen.
Using their vital force without restraint
leads to violence.
To grow old after reaching their prime
is contrary to the Tao.
What is contrary to the Tao soon perishes.

56

One who knows does not speak.
One who speaks does not know.

Remain quiet.
Guard the senses.
Blunt sharp edges.
Smooth the tangles.
Tone down radiance.
Unite with the dust.

This is called merging with the one.

Be not troubled by love.
Be not troubled by enemies.
Be not troubled by profit.
Be not troubled by loss.
Be not troubled by favor.
Be not troubled by disgrace.
Thus, one lives with honor.

57

Govern the state with integrity.
Lead the army with craftiness.
Rule the empire with inactivity.
How do I know this is true?
By what is within.

As laws and restrictions increase,
the people grow poorer.
As weapons increase,
the state grows troubled.
As cunning and cleverness increase,
events grow more alarming.
As laws and rules increase,
robbery becomes more common.

When the sage practices nonassertion,
the people reform themselves.
When the sage practices quietude,
the people develop righteousness.
When the sage practices inactivity,
the people become richer.
When the sage practices nondesire,
the people return to simplicity.

58

When the government avoids pretension,
the people will thrive.
When the government is interfering,
the people become dissatisfied.

Misery and happiness are intertwined.
Under misery happiness can be found.
Who can foresee what the future holds?
Disaster cannot be prevented.

The ordinary and extraordinary are intertwined.
Under the good the unfortunate can be found.
This cycle is bewildering and ongoing.

Therefore, the sage is:
Sharp but not piercing,
disciplined but not offensive,
straight but not restrictive,
and shining but not dazzling.

59

To govern the people and serve heaven,
there is nothing like restraint.
Restraint comes from early practice.

By early practice, one can accumulate virtue.
With an abundance of virtue,
everything can be overcome.

When everything can be overcome,
there are no limits.
Without limits, one can possess the Tao.

One who has possession of the Tao will endure.
This is called having deep roots and a strong stem.
This is the way of everlasting life and eternal vision.

60

Govern a country as you would cook small fish.
Do not handle them too much.

If the country is managed with Tao,
its evil spirits will be impotent.
Not only will the evil spirits be impotent,
its gods will not harm the people.
Not only will its gods not harm the people,
its sages will not harm the people.
When none will harm,
their virtues reinforce each other.

61

A great state is like a lowland to which all rivers flow.
Such a state is like the female who conquers the male
through yielding.
By yielding she becomes very still.

A great state yielding to a small state will conquer
the small state.
Conversely, a small state yielding to a great state will
conquer the great state.

Some yield for the purpose of winning.
Others win because they yield.

A great state's goal is to unite and feed its people.
A small state's goal is to be of service to its people.
In both cases, their goals are achieved through yielding.

62

The Tao is the refuge of the ten thousand things.
It is the good person's treasure.
It is the bad person's protection.

With fine words one can buy honor.
With honest conduct one can gain respect.

A bad person should not be rejected.
On the day the emperor is crowned and the ministers
are appointed, do not offer jade or a team of horses
but offer stillness and the eternal Tao.

Why do people prize the Tao?
Because when it is sought, it is found.
Sinners are forgiven their transgressions.
Therefore, the Tao is valued by the world.

63

Practice nonassertion.
Work without effort.
Taste the tasteless.
Attend the small.
Regard the few.

Replace hatred with virtue.

Approach the difficult when it is easy.
Undertake the great when it is small.

The most difficult tasks begin when easy.
The greatest tasks begin when small.

The sage avoids the great and, therefore,
achieves greatness.

Promises given lightly lack faith.
Easy things often include difficulties.

The sage avoids difficulties by regarding
everything as difficult.

64

What is still is easy to hold.
Before symptoms appear prevention is easy.
What is weak is easy to break.
The small is easy to scatter.

Attend to things before they develop.
Create order before disorder begins.
A large oak grows from a tiny acorn.
A tower is built brick by brick.
A journey of a thousand miles begins with a single step.

One who acts makes mistakes.
One who grasps loses.
Sages do not act, therefore, they do not make mistakes.
Sages do not grasp, therefore, they do not lose.
People often fail when nearing success.

To avoid failure, maintain as much care at the end of
a task as at the beginning.

Sages avoid desire.
They do not seek rare objects.
They choose not to be learned.
They seek the Tao when others pass it by.

Without interfering, sages are able to help the ten
thousand things find their own way.

65

In ancient times, those who knew the Tao
did not enlighten the people.
Instead, they used it to keep them simple.

If people are difficult to rule
it is because they are too clever.
Those who rule the state through cleverness
rob the state.
Those who avoid cleverness in ruling the state
bless the state.
One who knows these two things is a model.
To be a model is to have profound virtue.

Profound virtue is deep and far-reaching.
It leads all things to return to oneness.

66

Rivers can be kings of the hundred valleys
because of their position of lowliness.
For this reason, they can be kings
of the hundred valleys.

Therefore, sages who want to guide the people
must in their speech be beneath them.
Sages who want to lead the people
must in their person follow them.

Sages dwell above the people,
but the people do not feel their weight.
When sages lead the people,
the people feel no threat.

The world praises these sages
and does not tire of them.
Because sages do not compete with the people,
the people do not compete with them.

67

All the world calls me great, but I am unlike everyone else.
People are great because they do not resemble everyone else.
If they resemble everyone else, they would be insignificant.

I have three great treasures:
The first is compassion.
The second is frugality.
The third is humility.

The compassionate can be courageous.
The frugal can be generous.
The humble can be leaders.

If people abandon compassion and are courageous,
if they abandon frugality and are generous,
if they abandon humility and seek leadership,
they will surely die.

Compassion helps people win in case of attack.
Compassion helps people be strong in case of defense.
If heaven is to save people, it saves them through compassion.

68

One who excels at being a leader of soldiers is not violent.
One who excels at being a fighter is not angry.
One who excels in conquering the enemy is not vengeful.
One who excels in employing troops is humble.

This is called the virtue of not striving.
This is called using the ability of others.
This is called being in unity with the Tao.

69

A military strategist said:
"I must not act as the host but instead act as the guest.
Rather than advance an inch, it is better to retreat a foot."

This is called marching without seeming to move,
showing an arm without flexing a muscle,
being armed without weapons, and
presenting no opponent to the enemy.

Making light of the enemy is a great mistake.
Making light of the enemy is to lose what one values.

Therefore, when the battle begins,
one who shows sorrow is destined to conquer.

70

My words are easy to understand and practice,
yet no person can understand or practice them.

My words arise from nature.
My deeds arise from the Tao.
Because people do not understand my words and deeds,
they do not understand me.
I am obscure, therefore, I am valued.

Sages wear their jewels under common garments.

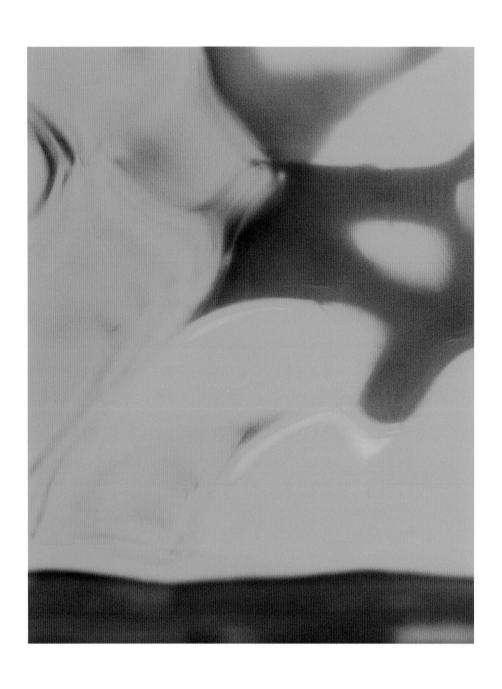

71

Knowing the unknowable is strength.
Avoiding knowledge is illness.

Only when we become sick of being ill
do we overcome illness.

Sages do not become ill.
They have become sick of illness,
therefore, they are not ill.

72

If people are not afraid of the harmful,
then their fears will be realized.

Do not restrict the lives of the people.
Do not hinder their means of livelihood.
Only when you cease to oppress them
will they cease to be wary of you.

Sages know themselves
but they do not show off this knowledge.
They have self-respect but they are not arrogant.
They choose the former and reject the latter.

73

Bravery combined with daring leads to death.
Bravery not combined with daring leads to life.
One kind of bravery is good,
the other kind of bravery is harmful.

Why are some things doomed by heaven?
Even the sage finds this question puzzling.

The Tao of heaven does not compete, yet it wins.
It does not speak, yet it responds.
It comes without being called.
Without aim, it achieves its purpose.

Heaven's net is cast over a vast area.
Its mesh is wide, yet nothing slips through.

74

If people are not afraid of death
you cannot frighten them with death.
We believe that those who break the law will fear death.
They are given the death penalty for their transgressions.
Who would presume to act in this way?

There is a master executioner in charge of death.
Trying to take the place of this master executioner
is like trying to take the place of a master carpenter.
If you take the place of a master carpenter,
you run the risk of hurting your hands.

75

Why are people hungry?
Because their rulers collect too many taxes.
Therefore, the people are hungry.
Why are the people hard to govern?
Because their rulers interfere.
Therefore, the people are hard to govern.
Why do people take death lightly?
Because their rulers cling to life too intensely.
Therefore, the people take death lightly.

One who does not seek after life
is wiser than one who values life.

76

At birth, people are tender and supple.
After death, they become hard and rigid.

During life, the ten thousand creatures and the
grasses and trees are tender and pliant.
After death, they become hard and dried out.

Thus, the hard and rigid are the companions of death.
The tender and supple are the companions of life.

Therefore, one who is strong in armaments will not win.
A tree that becomes rigid will die.

The rigid and strong will fail.
The pliant and weak will thrive.

77

The Tao is like bending a bow.
When the string is high, lower it.
When the string is low, raise it.
What is high must be subtracted from and
what is low must be added to.

The way of the Tao, therefore, is to reduce the excessive
and increase the deficient.

The way of the people is different.
They take from the deficient and give to the abundant.

Who is able to have such abundance
that they can offer it to the world?
Only students of the Tao.

Students of the Tao act but claim no credit.
They accomplish their tasks without dwelling on them.
They have no desire to display their worthiness.

78

Nothing in the world is softer or more delicate than water.
It cannot be surpassed in attacking the hard and the strong.
As a force of nature, it cannot be replaced.

The soft defeats the hard, the delicate defeats the strong.
This is known by all, but none practice it.

Therefore, the sage says:
Those who take upon themselves the disgrace of the state
are fit to rule the land.
Those who take upon themselves the misfortunes of the state
deserve to be the leaders of the state.

Such wisdom seems paradoxical.

79

When peace is made after great hatred,
some hatred is left behind.
How can this be reconciled?

Sages respect their part of a contract
and make no demands on others.
Virtuous people honor their obligations.
Those without virtue focus on the mistakes of others.

The Tao has no favorites,
but it always assists the side of the good.

80

Let countries be small and uncrowded.
Encourage leaders not to use their power.
Help the people grieve death.
Avoid traveling in ships and carriages
and be content to stay home.
Ask that weapons not be displayed.

Replace complicated methods with the simple
device of knotted thread.
Find satisfaction in food and pleasure in clothes.
Find comfort in home and delight in the
community's customs.

Neighboring states might be in view of one another.
The roosters and dogs from one state might be
heard in the next state.
Nevertheless, the people are content to grow
old and die without visiting neighboring states.

81

True words are not always agreeable
and agreeable words are not always true.
Good people do not argue
and those who argue are not good.
Wise people are not always learned
and learned people are not always wise.

Sages do not hoard.
The more they do for others,
the more they do for themselves.
The more they give to others,
the more they accumulate for themselves.

The way of the Tao is to help people,
not to hurt them.
The way of the Tao is to act without competition.

Bibliography

Blofeld, John. *Taoism: The Road to Immortality.* Boulder, Colo.: Shambhala, 1978.

Carus, Paul. *The Canon of Reason and Virtue.* LaSalle, Ill.: Open Court, 1945. First published in 1898.

Chan, Wing-Tsit. *The Way of Lao Tzu.* Indianapolis and New York: Bobbs-Merrill, 1963.

Cleary, Thomas. *The Essential Tao: An Initiation into the Heart of Taoism.* New York: HarperCollins, 1991.

Lau, D. C. *Tao Te Ching.* Harmondsworth, England: Penguin Books, 1963.

Lin Yutang. *The Wisdom of Laotse.* New York: Random House, 1948.

Waley, Arthur. *The Way and Its Power: A Study of the Tao Te Ching and Its Place in Chinese Thought.* London: George Allen & Unwin, 1934.

About the Author/Photographer

Betsy Wyckoff worked for twenty-five years as a development editor for several New York City publishers. Now a full-time writer, her interest in the Tao began in college and has extended over her lifetime. Her most recent books include *Indian Summer: A Native American View of Nature* and *Talking Apes and Dancing Bees: Intelligence, Emotions and Other Marvels of the Animal Kingdom.*

Her photography first appeared in a group show at the Sierra Club's New York City office in the 1960s. Her work over the next thirty years has been shown in numerous galleries and has appeared as cover and internal art in a variety of publications, including *Indian Summer.*

Betsy Wyckoff lives in New York City.